PYTHON OBJECT

ORIENTED

PROGRAMMING

FOR BEGINNERS

... Learn the Secrets of Clean, Reusable Code with Python's Object-Oriented Paradigm - Build Powerful Python Applications the Smart Way

DARREN ADAMS

DEDICATION

I specially dedicate this book to you. Yes, you for taking out time and money to acquire knowledge.

Table of Contents

Chapter 1: Introduction to Object-Oriented Programming in Python

What is Object-Oriented Programming (OOP)?

Object-Oriented Programming (OOP) is a programming paradigm that organizes software design around data, or objects, rather than functions and logic. An object can be thought of as a self-contained unit that contains both data and procedures to manipulate that data. This approach models real-world entities more intuitively and allows for the creation of scalable and maintainable software.

OOP revolves around four key principles: **Encapsulation**, **Abstraction**, **Inheritance**, and **Polymorphism**. These principles help reduce redundancy, increase reusability, and simplify complex systems.

Procedural vs. OOP: Key Differences

Procedural programming is a linear top-down approach where tasks are completed in a sequence using procedures or functions. While this method is effective for smaller programs, it becomes difficult to manage and scale as the application grows.

Feature	Procedural Programming	Object-Oriented Programming
Structure	Functions and procedures	Classes and objects
Data Handling	Data is separate from functions	Data and methods are encapsulated within objects
Reusability	Less reusable	Highly reusable via inheritance and composition
Scalability	Hard to manage large codebases	Easier to manage and scale

In contrast, OOP provides a more modular and organized way of programming by bundling data and the methods that operate on that data into objects. This modularity supports team collaboration and code maintenance.

Why OOP Matters in Real-World Software Development

In real-world software projects, complexity is inevitable. As systems grow, the need for maintainable, reusable, and scalable code becomes critical. OOP provides:

- **Modularity**: Divide large systems into smaller, manageable pieces.
- **Reusability**: Use inheritance and composition to reduce redundancy.
- **Maintainability**: Isolate changes to individual classes, reducing side effects.
- **Flexibility**: Through polymorphism, different object types can be treated uniformly.

Consider a banking system. With OOP, you can create classes such as `Account`, `Customer`, and `Transaction`, each encapsulating their behavior and state. This results in clearer, more intuitive code.

Brief History and Philosophy of Python's OOP Model

Python, developed by Guido van Rossum and first released in 1991, was built with readability and simplicity in mind. While it is a multi-paradigm language (supporting procedural, functional, and object-oriented styles), Python embraces OOP as a core part of its identity.

In Python, everything is an object—even primitive types like integers and strings. The class-based OOP system in Python is designed to be intuitive, flexible, and dynamically typed. Unlike Java or C++, Python does not require verbose syntax to create classes, making it a great choice for beginners.

Example: In Python, defining a class is as simple as:

```
class Dog:
    def bark(self):
        print("Woof!")
```

Before diving into OOP, you need a proper development setup. Here's a quick guide to get you started:

1. Install Python:

- Download and install Python from https://www.python.org.
- Ensure you add Python to your system's PATH during installation.

2. Choose an IDE or Code Editor:

- Recommended: Visual Studio Code, PyCharm, Sublime Text
- For beginners, VS Code is lightweight and extensible.

3. Create a Project Directory:

```
mkdir oop_python_basics
cd oop_python_basics
```

4. Create Your First Script:

```
touch main.py
```

Now you're ready to start coding in OOP-style Python.

Let's write a simple program that defines a class and creates an object from it.

```python
# main.py
class Person:
    def __init__(self, name, age):
        self.name = name
        self.age = age

    def greet(self):
        print(f"Hello, my name is {self.name} and I am {self.age} years old.")

# Creating an object
john = Person("John", 30)
john.greet()
```

Explanation:

- `class Person`: defines a class named `Person`.
- `__init__` is a special method called a constructor. It initializes the object's attributes.
- `self` refers to the current instance of the class.
- `greet` is a method that prints a message.
- `john = Person("John", 30)` creates an object of type `Person`.

- `john.greet()` calls the `greet` method on the object.

This foundational code introduces how classes work in Python. You can now begin building more complex systems using similar principles.

Summary

In this chapter, we covered the foundational concepts of Object-Oriented Programming in Python. We discussed the benefits of OOP over procedural programming, explored how Python's object model works, and set up our development environment. Finally, we created our first class and object.

As you proceed to the next chapters, you'll dive deeper into class design, encapsulation, inheritance, and other OOP concepts— equipping you with the tools to write clean, reusable, and maintainable Python code.

Chapter 2: Classes and Objects - The Foundation of OOP

Object-Oriented Programming (OOP) is at the core of modern software development, and Python, though a multiparadigm language, fully embraces the OOP paradigm. If you're aiming to become a proficient Python developer, mastering the principles of classes and objects is non-negotiable. This chapter introduces you to the foundational building blocks of OOP: classes and objects. Whether you're building command-line tools, web apps, or AI systems, understanding how to effectively use these components will shape the way you write Python code.

Understanding Classes: Blueprints of Objects

Think of a **class** as a template or blueprint. Just like an architect designs a building blueprint before any actual house is built, a class defines the structure and behavior of the objects created from it.

Let's consider an example:

```python
CopyEdit
class Car:
    pass
```

This `Car` class doesn't do much yet, but it serves as a template. From this class, we can create individual **objects** or **instances**, which represent real-world cars.

Classes encapsulate **attributes** (data) and **methods** (functions that define behavior). Together, they define what an object knows and what it can do.

Creating and Instantiating Objects

Once a class is defined, you can create objects from it—this process is called **instantiation**. Each object is an independent entity that follows the blueprint of the class.

```python
CopyEdit
class Car:
```

```
    def __init__(self, make, model,
year):
        self.make = make
        self.model = model
        self.year = year

my_car = Car("Toyota", "Corolla",
2020)
```

In this example, `my_car` is an object (or instance) of the `Car` class. It has its own `make`, `model`, and `year`—independent of any other `Car` objects we may create.

Each time we call `Car(...)`, we're constructing a new object with its own attributes. This is the essence of object-oriented programming: modeling the real world using self-contained units of code.

Attributes vs Methods: Data vs Behavior

A class typically contains two major components:

1. **Attributes** – These are variables that store the state or properties of an object.
2. **Methods** – These are functions defined inside a class that define what actions an object can perform.

Let's add a method to our `Car` class:

```python
CopyEdit
class Car:
    def __init__(self, make, model, year):
        self.make = make
        self.model = model
        self.year = year

    def start_engine(self):
        print(f"The {self.year} {self.make} {self.model}'s engine has started.")
```

Here, `start_engine()` is a method that describes what the car can do. It interacts with the object's attributes and performs a specific task.

You can call this method like so:

```python
CopyEdit
my_car.start_engine()
```

This will output:

```rust
CopyEdit
The 2020 Toyota Corolla's engine has started.
```

In KDP-relevant technical books, such clear examples help readers visualize concepts and immediately apply them, boosting engagement and comprehension.

Using the __init__ Constructor Method

Python provides a special method called __init__ (short for "initialize"), which is automatically called when a new object is created. It is the **constructor** of the class.

Its primary purpose is to initialize the object's attributes with specific values. Without __init__, objects would be instantiated without any meaningful data.

Let's revisit the Car class to illustrate the constructor:

```python
CopyEdit
def __init__(self, make, model, year):
    self.make = make
    self.model = model
    self.year = year
```

The __init__ method takes self (more on this soon) as its first argument, followed by other parameters. When we create a `Car` object, we pass values that get assigned to the object's attributes.

You can think of the `__init__` method as the place where objects "come to life" with actual data.

The `self` Keyword Explained

One of the most misunderstood elements for Python OOP beginners is the `self` keyword. Let's demystify it.

In Python, `self` represents the instance of the class. It allows access to the attributes and methods of that object. Whenever you define a method inside a class, it must take `self` as its first argument.

Here's an intuitive breakdown:

```python
CopyEdit
class Dog:
    def __init__(self, name):
        self.name = name

    def bark(self):
        print(f"{self.name} says
woof!")
```

Now, when we create a `Dog` object:

```python
CopyEdit
my_dog = Dog("Buddy")
my_dog.bark()
```

The `self.name = name` line assigns the `name` to the specific object being created. When `bark()` is called, it knows which dog's name to use because of `self`.

Important note: You don't pass the `self` argument when calling the method—Python handles that automatically.

This structure supports encapsulation, one of the pillars of OOP, by keeping data and behavior bound to the specific instance of the class.

Best Practices for Naming and Class Design

Following best practices when designing classes ensures your code is readable, maintainable, and scalable. Here are some guidelines every beginner (and even seasoned coder) should remember:

1. Use PascalCase for Class Names

Class names should start with an uppercase letter and follow the PascalCase convention:

```python
CopyEdit
class ElectricCar:
    pass
```

2. Use descriptive names for clarity

Avoid vague names like `Thing` or `Object1`. Instead, opt for meaningful names that reflect the purpose of the class.

```python
CopyEdit
class InvoiceProcessor:
    pass
```

3. Limit each class to a single responsibility

A class should do one thing and do it well. If your class starts doing too much, consider breaking it into multiple classes. This is in line with the **Single Responsibility Principle**.

4. Keep attributes private if necessary

While Python does not enforce strict access modifiers like Java or C++, it's a good habit to prefix private variables with an underscore:

```python
CopyEdit
class BankAccount:
    def __init__(self, balance):
        self._balance = balance
```

This signals to other developers that `_balance` is for internal use only.

5. Use methods to interact with attributes

Provide methods to get or update attributes rather than accessing them directly. This promotes encapsulation.

```python
CopyEdit
class BankAccount:
    def __init__(self, balance):
        self._balance = balance

    def deposit(self, amount):
```

```python
        self._balance += amount

    def get_balance(self):
        return self._balance
```

6. Comment your classes and methods

Always document your code using docstrings. This is especially important for KDP publications, as it improves code readability in print and eBook formats.

```python
python
CopyEdit
class Student:
    """
    Represents a student with a
name and GPA.
    """

    def __init__(self, name, gpa):
        """
        Initializes the student
with name and GPA.
        """
        self.name = name
        self.gpa = gpa
```

Summary

In this chapter, we've laid the essential groundwork for object-oriented programming in Python. You've learned that:

- A **class** is a blueprint for creating objects.
- An **object** is an instance of a class with its own attributes and behaviors.
- The `__init__` method is the constructor that initializes new objects.
- The `self` keyword refers to the current object and is used to access its data and methods.
- Attributes store **data**, while methods define **behavior**.
- Good naming and design practices help make your code clean, maintainable, and professional.

In the next chapter, we'll explore **Encapsulation, Inheritance, and Polymorphism**, diving deeper into how these OOP principles empower you to write scalable and modular code in Python.

By building on the concepts from this chapter, you'll soon be developing robust Python programs that are not only functional but also elegant.

Chapter 3: Encapsulation and Data Hiding

In the world of object-oriented programming, **encapsulation** is one of the key pillars that ensures your code is secure, maintainable, and modular. It provides a way to bundle data (attributes) and the methods that operate on that data into a single unit, usually a class. This chapter dives deep into how Python implements encapsulation, how data hiding works, and why it is crucial in both small scripts and enterprise-scale applications.

By the end of this chapter, you'll understand how to structure your Python classes for secure data handling, maintain clear separation of concerns, and write code that's easier to debug and maintain.

Encapsulation is the practice of keeping the internal state of an object hidden from the outside world. It allows object attributes to be accessed and modified only through methods defined by the class. This gives you control over how data is accessed and changed, preventing unintended interference.

In simple terms, it's like storing your valuables in a locked box. Only someone with the key (methods) can access or modify the contents.

In Python, encapsulation helps you:

- Prevent accidental modification of data
- Hide internal implementation details
- Simplify the public interface of your class
- Promote maintainability and scalability

Let's look at an example of encapsulation in action.

```python
CopyEdit
class Employee:
    def __init__(self, name,
salary):
        self.name = name
        self.__salary = salary  #
private attribute

    def get_salary(self):
        return self.__salary

    def set_salary(self, amount):
        if amount > 0:
            self.__salary = amount
```

In the example above, `__salary` is hidden
from direct access. It can only be accessed
or modified through the `get_salary()` and
`set_salary()` methods.

Public, Protected, and Private Members in Python

Python provides a naming convention, rather
than strict access modifiers like some other
languages. However, these conventions are
respected and widely followed.

1. Public Members

These are accessible from anywhere, both inside and outside the class.

```python
CopyEdit
class Person:
    def __init__(self, name):
        self.name = name   # public
```

You can access it directly:

```python
CopyEdit
p = Person("Alice")
print(p.name)   # Output: Alice
```

2. Protected Members

These are indicated with a single underscore prefix _. They are **not truly private**, but signal to developers that these members should be treated as non-public.

```python
CopyEdit
class Student:
    def __init__(self, name):
        self._name = name   #
protected
```

You *can* access _name, but you're **not supposed to** unless you're within the class or a subclass.

3. Private Members

These are denoted by two leading underscores __. Python applies name mangling to make them harder to access from outside the class.

```python
CopyEdit
class Account:
    def __init__(self):
        self.__balance = 1000  #
private
```

Trying to access __balance directly will raise an error:

```python
CopyEdit
a = Account()
print(a.__balance)  #
AttributeError
```

But technically, it's still accessible via name mangling:

```python
CopyEdit
```

```
print(a._Account__balance)   # Not
recommended
```

Use private attributes when you want to strictly control how data is accessed or updated.

Using Getter and Setter Methods

Encapsulation shines when you use **getter** and **setter** methods to access or update private variables. This provides validation and control over data manipulation.

Let's expand our Employee example:

```python
CopyEdit
class Employee:
    def __init__(self, name,
salary):
        self.__name = name
        self.__salary = salary

    def get_salary(self):
        return self.__salary

    def set_salary(self, value):
        if value < 0:
```

```
          raise
ValueError("Salary cannot be
negative")
        self.__salary = value
```

This pattern is important when your class needs to enforce constraints. It keeps your data **safe** and your codebase **robust**.

With getter/setter methods, you're applying a principle called **information hiding**, shielding sensitive parts of your program from unintended interference.

Property Decorators (`@property`) for Clean Access

Python takes encapsulation one step further with the `@property` decorator. It allows you to create **readable and Pythonic access** to private attributes, while still applying validation and logic.

Here's a cleaner version of the `Employee` class using `@property`:

```python
CopyEdit
```

```python
class Employee:
    def __init__(self, name, salary):
        self.__name = name
        self.__salary = salary

    @property
    def salary(self):
        return self.__salary

    @salary.setter
    def salary(self, value):
        if value < 0:
            raise ValueError("Salary must be a positive number")
        self.__salary = value
```

Now, you can interact with the `salary` attribute as if it were public:

```python
python
CopyEdit
emp = Employee("John", 5000)
print(emp.salary)          # Accesses via getter
emp.salary = 6000          # Updates via setter
```

This approach combines the **simplicity of public access** with the **control of private encapsulation**, offering the best of both worlds.

In KDP publications, this is a great example to present in both code blocks and real-world analogies. It resonates well with both beginners and professionals.

Real-World Use Case: Bank Account Class with Data Hiding

Let's build a realistic example to show encapsulation in a real-world scenario: managing a **bank account**.

```python
CopyEdit
class BankAccount:
    def __init__(self, owner, balance=0):
        self.owner = owner
        self.__balance = balance

    @property
    def balance(self):
        return self.__balance

    def deposit(self, amount):
        if amount > 0:
            self.__balance += amount
        else:
```

```
            raise
ValueError("Deposit amount must be
positive")

    def withdraw(self, amount):
        if 0 < amount <=
self.__balance:
            self.__balance -=
amount
        else:
            raise
ValueError("Insufficient funds or
invalid amount")
```

Usage:

```python
CopyEdit
acc = BankAccount("Alice", 1000)
acc.deposit(500)
print(acc.balance)   # 1500
acc.withdraw(200)
print(acc.balance)   # 1300
```

Here, __balance is hidden from direct access, ensuring that deposits and withdrawals are validated through the class's own logic.

This pattern is widely used in fintech, payroll systems, and e-commerce platforms—anywhere money is involved.

As your Python projects grow in
complexity, encapsulation becomes a
strategic advantage. Here's why:

✅ Better Code Maintainability

Changes to how data is stored or validated
don't affect external code. You can change
the internal logic without rewriting code that
uses your class.

✅ Prevents Unauthorized Access

Encapsulation protects critical data by
enforcing rules through methods. No
external code can change your object's state
in a harmful or inconsistent way.

✅ Easier Debugging and Testing

When bugs occur, encapsulated components
are easier to isolate and test. You know
where data changes are happening—only in
controlled locations.

✅ Improved Reusability

Encapsulated classes are self-contained. They can be reused in different parts of your project or in entirely new projects without conflict.

✅ Cleaner API Design

Exposing only the necessary methods and hiding internal logic helps you create a cleaner and easier-to-understand API.

✅ Supports Principle of Least Privilege

Encapsulation ensures that parts of your code only have access to the information they need—no more, no less. This is a key practice in secure software design.

Summary

Encapsulation is much more than just a buzzword. It's a powerful concept that makes your Python code safer, more maintainable, and more professional. Here's what you've learned in this chapter:

- Encapsulation groups related data and behavior into a single unit (class).
- Public, protected, and private members are defined by naming conventions.
- Getter and setter methods offer controlled access to internal attributes.
- Python's `@property` decorator enables cleaner and more intuitive syntax.
- Real-world examples like a bank account demonstrate the value of data hiding.
- Encapsulation offers real advantages in terms of security, maintainability, and modularity—especially in large applications.

In the next chapter, we'll explore **inheritance**, another foundational concept that allows your classes to reuse code and extend functionality.

Chapter 4: Inheritance – Reusing Code the Smart Way

In software development, efficiency is key. One way to improve efficiency is by **reusing** code, and in object-oriented programming (OOP), **inheritance** is the mechanism that allows you to do just that. Inheritance enables new classes to inherit the attributes and behaviors of existing ones, facilitating the creation of specialized classes with minimal effort. In this chapter, you'll learn how to use inheritance to write cleaner, more maintainable code while adhering to the DRY (Don't Repeat Yourself) principle.

By the end of this chapter, you will understand how to create base and derived classes, override methods, use the `super()` function, and explore more advanced inheritance concepts like multiple inheritance and method resolution order (MRO).

In OOP, **inheritance** is a mechanism where a class (called a **derived** or **child** class) can inherit attributes and methods from another class (called a **base** or **parent** class). This allows you to create new classes that extend or modify the functionality of existing ones without having to rewrite the code.

The main reasons to use inheritance are:

- **Code Reusability**: Instead of writing the same code again, you can reuse existing code from the base class, improving productivity and reducing errors.
- **Maintainability**: Changes made to the parent class can automatically propagate to child classes, making it easier to maintain and update code.
- **Extensibility**: Child classes can extend the functionality of the parent class by adding new features or overriding existing ones.

For example, imagine you're building a library management system. Instead of creating separate classes for every type of item in the library (book, magazine, DVD), you can create a generic `LibraryItem` class and then inherit from it to create specific item types.

Creating Base and Derived Classes

Creating base and derived classes in Python is straightforward. Let's start with a simple example:

```python
CopyEdit
class Animal:
    def __init__(self, name):
        self.name = name

    def speak(self):
        print(f"{self.name} makes a sound")

class Dog(Animal):
    def __init__(self, name, breed):
        super().__init__(name)  # Call the parent class's __init__ method
        self.breed = breed

    def speak(self):
        print(f"{self.name} barks")
```

Here, the `Animal` class is the **base class** (or parent class), and the `Dog` class is the **derived class** (or child class). Notice that the `Dog` class inherits the `speak()` method from the `Animal` class but also overrides it to provide a more specific implementation.

- The `super()` function is used to call the parent class's constructor (`__init__()` method) from within the derived class.
- The derived class can override any methods from the base class to modify or extend their behavior.

Overriding Parent Methods

When a derived class overrides a method, it provides a new implementation that replaces the method in the parent class. This is useful when you want to retain the same method name but change its behavior in the child class.

Let's modify the `Dog` class to demonstrate method overriding:

```python
CopyEdit
class Animal:
    def __init__(self, name):
        self.name = name

    def speak(self):
        print(f"{self.name} makes a
sound")

class Dog(Animal):
    def __init__(self, name,
breed):
        super().__init__(name)
        self.breed = breed

    def speak(self):
        print(f"{self.name} barks
loudly!")
```

Now, if you create an instance of `Dog` and call `speak()`, you'll see the new behavior:

```python
CopyEdit
my_dog = Dog("Max", "Golden
Retriever")
my_dog.speak()   # Output: Max barks
loudly!
```

While the `Animal` class had a general `speak()` method, the `Dog` class provides a more specific implementation, demonstrating the power of overriding.

The `super()` Function and How to Use It Effectively

The `super()` function is crucial when you want to call a method from the parent class. It's particularly useful in the constructor (`__init__()`), but you can also use it to call other parent class methods.

Here's a deeper look at how `super()` works:

```python
CopyEdit
class Parent:
    def __init__(self, value):
        self.value = value

    def show_value(self):
        print(f"Value from Parent:
{self.value}")

class Child(Parent):
    def __init__(self, value,
extra_value):
        super().__init__(value)  #
Calls Parent's __init__ method
        self.extra_value =
extra_value

    def show_value(self):
        super().show_value()  #
Calls Parent's show_value method
```

```
        print(f"Value from Child:
{self.extra_value}")
```

Now, when you create a `Child` object and call `show_value()`, you get output from both the parent and the child class:

```python
python
CopyEdit
child = Child(10, 20)
child.show_value()
# Output:
# Value from Parent: 10
# Value from Child: 20
```

In this example, the `super()` function ensures that the `Child` class can call and extend functionality from the `Parent` class without duplicating code.

Real-World Scenario: Building a Vehicle Hierarchy

Let's now consider a real-world use case for inheritance. Suppose you're designing a **vehicle** hierarchy. All vehicles share some common features (like having a `make` and `model`), but different types of vehicles also have specific features. By using inheritance, you can build a hierarchy where common features are stored in a base class, and specialized features are added in derived classes.

```python
CopyEdit
class Vehicle:
    def __init__(self, make, model):
        self.make = make
        self.model = model

    def drive(self):
        print(f"The {self.make} {self.model} is driving.")

class Car(Vehicle):
    def __init__(self, make, model, num_doors):
        super().__init__(make, model)
        self.num_doors = num_doors

    def drive(self):
        print(f"The {self.make} {self.model} car is driving.")

class Truck(Vehicle):
    def __init__(self, make, model, payload_capacity):
        super().__init__(make, model)
        self.payload_capacity = payload_capacity

    def drive(self):
        print(f"The {self.make} {self.model} truck is driving with
```

a payload of
{self.payload_capacity} tons.")

Now, you can create instances of `Car` and `Truck` and use the `drive()` method:

```python
CopyEdit
car = Car("Toyota", "Corolla", 4)
car.drive()  # Output: The Toyota
Corolla car is driving.

truck = Truck("Ford", "F-150", 2)
truck.drive()  # Output: The Ford
F-150 truck is driving with a
payload of 2 tons.
```

In this case, `Vehicle` is the base class, and `Car` and `Truck` are derived classes. The base class contains common attributes and methods, while the derived classes introduce unique features for each type of vehicle.

Multiple Inheritance and the Method Resolution Order (MRO)

Python supports **multiple inheritance**, where a class can inherit from more than one parent class. While this is powerful, it also requires careful design to ensure that the method resolution order (MRO) is handled properly. The MRO determines the order in which classes are searched when looking for a method.

Here's an example of multiple inheritance:

```python
CopyEdit
class A:
    def speak(self):
        print("Class A speaking")

class B:
    def speak(self):
        print("Class B speaking")

class C(A, B):
    pass
```

In this case, C inherits from both A and B. Python will look for methods in the classes in the order they are listed. So, C will first search A and then B:

```python
CopyEdit
obj = C()
obj.speak()  # Output: Class A speaking
```

To understand how Python resolves method calls in multiple inheritance, you can use the `mro()` method:

```python
CopyEdit
print(C.mro())
```

This will output the method resolution order:

```kotlin
CopyEdit
[<class '__main__.C'>, <class
'__main__.A'>, <class
'__main__.B'>, <class 'object'>]
```

This shows that Python looks for methods in C, then A, and finally B.

Summary

Inheritance is a powerful concept in OOP that allows you to reuse and extend existing code, promoting both efficiency and maintainability. In this chapter, you've learned:

- **Inheritance** enables child classes to inherit attributes and methods from a parent class.
- **Method overriding** allows child classes to provide specific implementations for inherited methods.
- The `super()` function is a tool for calling parent class methods.
- A **real-world vehicle hierarchy** can be designed using inheritance.
- **Multiple inheritance** lets you inherit from more than one class, and the **method resolution order (MRO)** dictates how Python searches for methods.

In the next chapter, we'll explore **polymorphism**, a concept that lets objects of different classes be treated as instances of the same class, helping you write more flexible code.

Chapter 5: Polymorphism and Duck Typing in Python

Polymorphism is one of the most important concepts in object-oriented programming (OOP), and Python implements it in a very flexible and intuitive way. In this chapter, you will explore what polymorphism is, how it works in Python, and how you can leverage it to write cleaner, more maintainable code. Additionally, we'll delve into Python's unique approach to polymorphism through **duck typing**, a feature that allows objects to be treated based on their behavior rather than their type.

By the end of this chapter, you'll understand the core principles of polymorphism, how method overloading and overriding differ, and how to apply these concepts in real-world scenarios like shape drawing and architecture design.

Understanding Polymorphism: Many Forms, One Interface

Polymorphism is derived from Greek words meaning "many forms." In OOP, polymorphism allows objects of different classes to be treated as objects of a common superclass. It enables the same interface to be used for different data types, allowing the same operation to behave differently based on the object's type.

In simple terms, polymorphism means that different classes can share the same method name, but the implementation of that method can vary depending on the class that invokes it.

For example, you can have multiple classes—Dog, Cat, Bird—all implementing a speak() method. While the method name is the same, each class provides its own implementation of how the animal speaks.

```python
CopyEdit
class Dog:
    def speak(self):
        print("Woof!")

class Cat:
    def speak(self):
        print("Meow!")

class Bird:
    def speak(self):
        print("Tweet!")
```

Now, we can create instances of these classes and call the speak() method:

```python
CopyEdit
animals = [Dog(), Cat(), Bird()]

for animal in animals:
    animal.speak()  # Output: Woof!
Meow! Tweet!
```

In this example, we have three different classes, all using the same method name, `speak()`, but with different behaviors. This is the essence of polymorphism.

Method Overloading vs Method Overriding

In OOP, two common forms of polymorphism are **method overloading** and **method overriding**. Understanding these differences is key to using polymorphism effectively.

1. Method Overloading

Method overloading occurs when you have multiple methods with the same name but different parameters (number or type). Python does not support method overloading in the traditional sense like languages such as Java or C++. In Python, the last defined method with a particular name will overwrite previous ones. However, you can mimic overloading by using default arguments or variable-length arguments.

For example:

```python
CopyEdit
class Calculator:
    def add(self, a, b=0, c=0):
        return a + b + c

calc = Calculator()
print(calc.add(1))        # Output: 1
print(calc.add(1, 2))     # Output: 3
print(calc.add(1, 2, 3))  # Output: 6
```

Here, the add() method is overloaded with default values for the parameters. Based on how many arguments are passed, the method behaves differently.

2. Method Overriding

Method overriding occurs when a subclass provides its own implementation of a method that is already defined in its parent class. This is a core feature of polymorphism because it allows a subclass to alter the behavior of an inherited method.

Example:

```python
CopyEdit
class Animal:
    def speak(self):
        print("Some sound")

class Dog(Animal):
    def speak(self):
        print("Woof!")

class Cat(Animal):
    def speak(self):
        print("Meow!")
```

In this case, the `Dog` and `Cat` classes override the `speak()` method inherited from `Animal` to provide their own implementations.

One of Python's most powerful features is its **dynamic typing**, which is a core enabler of **duck typing**. Duck typing allows Python to focus on what an object **can do**, rather than what it **is**. In other words, if an object implements the methods and behaviors required by a certain context, Python allows it to be treated as the correct type, even if it doesn't explicitly inherit from a particular class or implement an interface.

The term "duck typing" comes from the saying, "If it looks like a duck and quacks like a duck, then it probably is a duck."

Here's a practical example of duck typing in Python:

```python
CopyEdit
class Dog:
    def speak(self):
        print("Woof!")

class Cat:
    def speak(self):
        print("Meow!")
```

```
def make_animal_speak(animal):
    animal.speak()

# Both Dog and Cat objects can be
passed to make_animal_speak
function
make_animal_speak(Dog())   # Output:
Woof!
make_animal_speak(Cat())   # Output:
Meow!
```

In this example, even though Dog and Cat
are different classes, Python treats them the
same as long as they have a speak()
method. There's no need for explicit
inheritance or interfaces, showcasing the
flexibility of duck typing.

Practical Example: Shape Drawing with Polymorphic Classes

Let's create a real-world example using
polymorphism. Suppose we are building a
graphics program where we need to draw
various shapes. Each shape will have a
draw() method, but the implementation of
the draw() method will differ for each
shape. Here's how we can structure it using
polymorphism:

```python
CopyEdit
class Shape:
    def draw(self):
        raise
NotImplementedError("Subclasses
must implement this method")

class Circle(Shape):
    def draw(self):
        print("Drawing a Circle")

class Square(Shape):
    def draw(self):
        print("Drawing a Square")

class Triangle(Shape):
    def draw(self):
        print("Drawing a Triangle")
```

Now, let's create a list of shapes and iterate through it, calling the `draw()` method on each shape:

```python
CopyEdit
shapes = [Circle(), Square(),
Triangle()]

for shape in shapes:
    shape.draw()
```

This results in:

```css
```

```
CopyEdit
Drawing a Circle
Drawing a Square
Drawing a Triangle
```

Notice that the same `draw()` method is called for each shape, but the output is different based on the class. This demonstrates polymorphism, where a single interface (`draw()`) is used for different types of objects (shapes).

Interfaces and Abstract Base Classes Using `abc` Module

Python doesn't have traditional interfaces like other OOP languages (e.g., Java). However, you can simulate interfaces using **Abstract Base Classes (ABCs)**. The `abc` module in Python allows you to define abstract classes that cannot be instantiated directly. Abstract methods in these classes must be implemented by subclasses.

Here's an example using `abc`:

```python
CopyEdit
```

```
from abc import ABC, abstractmethod

class Shape(ABC):
    @abstractmethod
    def draw(self):
        pass

class Circle(Shape):
    def draw(self):
        print("Drawing a Circle")

class Square(Shape):
    def draw(self):
        print("Drawing a Square")
```

In this example, `Shape` is an abstract base class that defines an abstract `draw()` method. Both `Circle` and `Square` must implement the `draw()` method, or they will raise an error.

```
python
CopyEdit
circle = Circle()
circle.draw()  # Output: Drawing a
Circle
```

If we try to instantiate `Shape` directly, Python will raise an error:

```
python
CopyEdit
```

```
shape = Shape()  # TypeError: Can't
instantiate abstract class Shape
with abstract methods draw
```

Using ABCs ensures that subclasses implement necessary methods, providing a contract for your classes and enhancing polymorphism's reliability.

When and How to Use Polymorphism for Clean Architecture

Polymorphism is a powerful tool in building clean, scalable, and maintainable architectures. Here are some scenarios where polymorphism is particularly beneficial:

- **When you have many similar objects**: If you have multiple classes that share common behavior (e.g., `Shape` classes like `Circle`, `Square`, etc.), polymorphism allows you to treat them uniformly.
- **For extensibility**: Polymorphism allows you to easily add new types of objects (like new shapes) without modifying existing code. This is

particularly useful in systems that are constantly evolving.

- **For decoupling**: By using polymorphism, you can decouple the behavior of objects from their concrete types. This allows components of your system to be more flexible and easier to modify independently.

For instance, in a plugin-based architecture, polymorphism allows you to easily add new plugins without changing the core application logic.

Summary

In this chapter, you've learned about polymorphism and duck typing in Python, which are crucial concepts for writing flexible, maintainable, and scalable code:

- **Polymorphism** allows you to use the same interface for different object types, enabling flexible and reusable code.

- **Method overloading** and **method overriding** are two ways polymorphism manifests in Python.
- **Duck typing** allows objects to be used based on their behavior, not their explicit type.
- You explored a real-world example of polymorphism with shape drawing, showcasing the power of common interfaces and different implementations.
- **Abstract Base Classes (ABCs)** and the `abc` module enable you to enforce method implementation across subclasses, ensuring consistent behavior.

In the next chapter, we'll dive into **composition**, another design principle that complements inheritance and helps you write even more modular and maintainable code.

Chapter 6: Composition vs Inheritance

In object-oriented programming (OOP), two fundamental design principles often come into play when modeling the relationships between classes: **composition** and **inheritance**. While inheritance has been the go-to method for creating relationships between objects, composition is a powerful alternative that can offer more flexibility and better design in certain situations.

In this chapter, we will explore what composition is, how it differs from inheritance, and how to use both approaches to build cleaner and more flexible class systems. We'll also dive into real-life examples to help clarify when to use one approach over the other and how a hybrid approach can sometimes offer the best solution.

In OOP, **composition** is a design principle where one object contains or is composed of other objects, and those objects contribute functionality to the parent object. Composition represents a "has-a" relationship between objects. For example, a `Car` has an `Engine` and `Tires`.

On the other hand, **inheritance** is a design principle where one class (the child class) inherits the attributes and methods from another class (the parent class). Inheritance represents an "is-a" relationship. For example, a `Dog` is an `Animal`, and a `Dog` inherits behavior from the `Animal` class.

While inheritance is a natural way to extend the functionality of a class, composition offers a more flexible and modular alternative. Let's break down the core differences:

- **Inheritance**:
    - Represents an "is-a" relationship.

- A subclass is a specialized version of a parent class.
- Encourages hierarchy and extensibility.
- Can lead to tightly coupled systems that are harder to maintain if not used carefully.
- **Composition**:
  - Represents a "has-a" relationship.
  - An object is composed of other objects, and it delegates tasks to them.
  - Provides flexibility and better modularity.
  - Allows for changing or replacing parts of an object without affecting the entire class system.

In Python, both inheritance and composition are available as tools for building relationships, and each has its strengths and weaknesses. The challenge lies in knowing when to use each approach effectively.

The terms **"has-a"** and **"is-a"** relationships are key to understanding the difference between composition and inheritance.

- **"Is-a" relationship (Inheritance)**: This relationship is used to model a class that is a specialized version of another class. The child class inherits the behavior and properties of the parent class.
  - Example: A `Dog` is an `Animal`. This is an "is-a" relationship because a dog is a type of animal, so it makes sense for `Dog` to inherit from `Animal`.
- **"Has-a" relationship (Composition)**: This relationship models the concept where one object **has** another object, but it is not a specialized version of that object. Instead, it contains it as a part or a component.
  - Example: A `Car` has an `Engine` and `Tires`. This is a "has-a" relationship because the car is not a type of engine

or tire; rather, it is composed of those components.

Let's now examine both relationships with concrete examples in Python.

"Is-a" Relationship Example (Inheritance)

```python
CopyEdit
class Animal:
    def speak(self):
        print("Animal makes a sound")

class Dog(Animal):
    def speak(self):
        print("Dog barks")

dog = Dog()
dog.speak()  # Output: Dog barks
```

In this example, `Dog` inherits from `Animal`, establishing an "is-a" relationship. A `Dog` is an `Animal`, so it makes sense to use inheritance.

"Has-a" Relationship Example (Composition)

```python
CopyEdit
```

```
class Engine:
    def start(self):
        print("Engine starts")

class Tires:
    def inflate(self):
        print("Tires inflated")

class Car:
    def __init__(self, engine,
tires):
        self.engine = engine
        self.tires = tires

    def drive(self):
        self.engine.start()
        self.tires.inflate()
        print("Car is driving")

engine = Engine()
tires = Tires()
car = Car(engine, tires)
car.drive()  # Output: Engine
starts Tires inflated Car is
driving
```

In this case, a `Car` has an `Engine` and `Tires`, establishing a "has-a" relationship. The `Car` doesn't inherit from `Engine` or `Tires`; instead, it uses them to achieve its functionality.

Using Composition to Build Flexible Class Systems

Composition allows for more flexibility in class design compared to inheritance. This is because, with composition, you can replace parts of an object without modifying its core behavior. You can also create complex objects by combining simpler ones, making your code more modular and reusable.

For instance, consider a system that simulates various types of vehicles. Using composition, we can define a `Vehicle` class that contains components such as an `Engine`, `Transmission`, and `FuelTank`.

```python
CopyEdit
class Engine:
    def start(self):
        print("Engine started")

class Transmission:
    def shift(self):
        print("Transmission
shifted")

class FuelTank:
    def refuel(self):
        print("Fuel tank refilled")
```

```python
class Vehicle:
    def __init__(self, engine,
transmission, fuel_tank):
        self.engine = engine
        self.transmission =
transmission
        self.fuel_tank = fuel_tank

    def drive(self):
        self.engine.start()
        self.transmission.shift()
        self.fuel_tank.refuel()
        print("Vehicle is driving")

engine = Engine()
transmission = Transmission()
fuel_tank = FuelTank()

vehicle = Vehicle(engine,
transmission, fuel_tank)
vehicle.drive()
```

Here, we can easily swap the `Engine`, `Transmission`, or `FuelTank` with other implementations without changing the `Vehicle` class. This flexibility makes composition an ideal choice for building complex systems.

Real-Life Example: A Car Composed of Engine and Tires

To make the concept clearer, let's use a real-life analogy: a **Car**.

A car is not a specialized type of Engine or Tires; rather, it **has** an engine and tires as part of its design. This is a typical "has-a" relationship. The car can delegate tasks like starting the engine or inflating the tires to the respective components.

```python
CopyEdit
class Car:
    def __init__(self, engine, tires):
        self.engine = engine
        self.tires = tires

    def start(self):
        self.engine.start()

    def inflate_tires(self):
        self.tires.inflate()

class Engine:
    def start(self):
        print("Engine started")

class Tires:
    def inflate(self):
```

```
        print("Tires inflated")

# Composing a car object
engine = Engine()
tires = Tires()
my_car = Car(engine, tires)

my_car.start()          # Output:
Engine started
my_car.inflate_tires()  # Output:
Tires inflated
```

This model allows the flexibility to change
the car's components independently, such as
upgrading the engine or replacing the tires,
without affecting other parts of the system.

When to Prefer Composition Over Inheritance

While both inheritance and composition are
valuable tools, composition is often
preferred in the following situations:

1. **When you need flexibility**:
   Composition allows objects to be
   composed of other objects, making it
   easier to replace or modify
   components without changing the
   entire class structure.

2. **When you want to avoid a deep inheritance hierarchy**: Inheritance can lead to rigid and deep class hierarchies, making code harder to maintain. Composition helps avoid this problem by promoting a flat, modular structure.
3. **When the relationship is more "has-a" than "is-a"**: If the relationship between objects is better represented as one object containing another, composition is the better choice.

Hybrid Approach: Combining Both for Optimal Design

In many real-world applications, a hybrid approach using both composition and inheritance works best. You can use inheritance when the relationship is clearly "is-a" and composition when the relationship is "has-a." This combination allows you to take advantage of both patterns' strengths.

For example, you could have a `Car` that inherits from a `Vehicle` class (representing the "is-a" relationship) while also using composition to include an `Engine` and `Tires` (representing the "has-a" relationship).

```python
CopyEdit
class Vehicle:
    def drive(self):
        print("Vehicle is driving")

class Car(Vehicle):
    def __init__(self, engine,
tires):
        self.engine = engine
        self.tires = tires

    def start(self):
        self.engine.start()

    def inflate_tires(self):
        self.tires.inflate()

class Engine:
    def start(self):
        print("Engine started")

class Tires:
    def inflate(self):
        print("Tires inflated")

# Combining inheritance and
composition
engine = Engine()
tires = Tires()
car = Car(engine, tires)
```

```
car.drive()        # Output:
Vehicle is driving
car.start()        # Output:
Engine started
car.inflate_tires() # Output: Tires
inflated
```

This hybrid approach allows you to benefit from the extensibility of inheritance while maintaining the flexibility of composition.

Summary

In this chapter, we explored the differences between **composition** and **inheritance** in object-oriented programming:

- **Inheritance** represents an "is-a" relationship and is ideal for extending the functionality of a base class.
- **Composition** represents a "has-a" relationship and provides more flexibility by allowing objects to contain other objects as components.
- Composition is often preferable for creating flexible and modular systems, while inheritance is suitable

for modeling class hierarchies and extending behavior.

- A **hybrid approach** combining both inheritance and composition can be used for optimal design in complex systems.

By understanding when and how to use both techniques, you can create cleaner, more maintainable, and scalable code.

Chapter 7: Magic Methods and Operator Overloading

Python is a powerful, expressive language that allows you to interact with objects in intuitive and dynamic ways. One of the key features that make Python's object-oriented programming (OOP) so versatile is its support for **magic methods** (often referred to as **dunder** methods, due to the double underscores that surround them). These methods enable you to customize the behavior of objects, making them behave more like built-in Python data types.

In this chapter, we'll explore Python's magic methods, learn how to use them to enhance your classes, and dive into the concept of **operator overloading**, allowing custom behavior when using operators like +, -, and others on objects.

Introduction to Python's Dunder Methods

In Python, magic methods are special methods that allow you to define the behavior of objects when they interact with built-in Python functions or operators. These methods always have double underscores before and after their name, such as `__str__`, `__repr__`, and `__len__`. These methods are the foundation of Python's **object customization** and **operator overloading**.

Magic methods allow you to modify how objects behave with Python's built-in functions, like `print()`, `len()`, `str()`, and even arithmetic operators such as +, -, and *. By overriding these methods, you can make your objects interact with these functions and operators in a way that feels natural and intuitive for users of your class.

Let's explore some of the most common magic methods you'll use in Python development.

Common Magic Methods

__str__ and __repr__

The __str__ and __repr__ methods are used to define how an object is represented as a string. While they may seem similar, they serve different purposes.

- **__str__**: This method is intended to return a human-readable, informal string representation of an object. It's the method that gets called when you use print() or str() on an object.

```python
CopyEdit
class Car:
    def __init__(self, make, model):
        self.make = make
        self.model = model

    def __str__(self):
        return f"{self.make} {self.model}"

car = Car("Toyota", "Corolla")
print(car)  # Output: Toyota Corolla
```

- **`__repr__`**: This method is meant to return a more formal string representation of an object, often one that could be used to recreate the object using `eval()` or help with debugging. When you type an object into the interactive Python shell or use `repr()`, it calls this method.

```python
CopyEdit
class Car:
    def __init__(self, make,
model):
        self.make = make
        self.model = model

    def __repr__(self):
        return
f"Car(make='{self.make}',
model='{self.model}')"

car = Car("Toyota",
"Corolla")
print(repr(car))  # Output:
Car(make='Toyota',
model='Corolla')
```

The key difference is that `__str__` is used for user-friendly output, while `__repr__` is aimed at developers and debugging.

__len__

The __len__ method allows you to define
the behavior when the built-in `len()`
function is called on your object. This is
particularly useful if you want your object to
behave like a collection, such as a list or a
dictionary.

```python
CopyEdit
class MyList:
    def __init__(self, items):
        self.items = items

    def __len__(self):
        return len(self.items)

my_list = MyList([1, 2, 3, 4])
print(len(my_list))  # Output: 4
```

In this example, calling `len(my_list)`
triggers the __len__ method, returning the
length of the list.

__eq__

The __eq__ method allows you to define the
behavior for the equality operator `==`. When
you use `==` to compare two objects, Python
will check for equality using this method.

```python
CopyEdit
class Point:
    def __init__(self, x, y):
        self.x = x
        self.y = y

    def __eq__(self, other):
        return self.x == other.x
and self.y == other.y

point1 = Point(2, 3)
point2 = Point(2, 3)
point3 = Point(4, 5)

print(point1 == point2)   # Output:
True
print(point1 == point3)   # Output:
False
```

Here, we define how to compare two `Point` objects by comparing their `x` and `y` coordinates. If they are equal, the `__eq__` method returns `True`; otherwise, it returns `False`.

Customizing Object Behavior with Operator Overloading

Operator overloading in Python allows you to redefine the behavior of operators (e.g., +,

-, *, /) for objects of your class. This gives you the ability to write code that feels more Pythonic, as objects can be manipulated using familiar operators.

Overloading the + Operator

Let's say you have a class representing vectors and you want to add two vectors using the + operator. You can overload the + operator by implementing the __add__ method.

```python
CopyEdit
class Vector:
    def __init__(self, x, y):
        self.x = x
        self.y = y

    def __add__(self, other):
        return Vector(self.x +
other.x, self.y + other.y)

    def __repr__(self):
        return f"Vector({self.x},
{self.y})"

vector1 = Vector(2, 3)
vector2 = Vector(4, 5)
vector3 = vector1 + vector2
```

```
print(vector3)   # Output: Vector(6,
8)
```

In this case, the + operator is used to add two `Vector` objects, and the `__add__` method defines how this operation should behave. As a result, `vector1 + vector2` creates a new `Vector` object with the sum of the corresponding `x` and `y` values.

Overloading Other Operators

You can overload many other operators using their corresponding magic methods. Some common ones include:

- `__sub__` for subtraction (-)
- `__mul__` for multiplication (*)
- `__truediv__` for division (/)
- `__floordiv__` for floor division (//)
- `__mod__` for modulo (%)

Here's an example of overloading the * operator for a `Matrix` class:

```python
CopyEdit
class Matrix:
    def __init__(self, data):
        self.data = data
```

```python
    def __mul__(self, other):
        return Matrix([[sum(a * b
for a, b in zip(row, col)) for col
in zip(*other.data)] for row in
self.data])

    def __repr__(self):
        return
f"Matrix({self.data})"

matrix1 = Matrix([[1, 2], [3, 4]])
matrix2 = Matrix([[5, 6], [7, 8]])
result = matrix1 * matrix2

print(result)  # Output:
Matrix([[19, 22], [43, 50]])
```

In this example, the * operator is overloaded to perform matrix multiplication. The __mul__ method is responsible for defining how the multiplication should be handled for Matrix objects.

Best Practices for Implementing Magic Methods

While magic methods provide powerful customization options, they should be used thoughtfully. Here are a few best practices for implementing them:

1. **Clarity over complexity**:
   Overloading magic methods should make your objects more intuitive and easier to use. Avoid creating overly complex implementations that could confuse users of your class.
2. **Consistency**: Stick to the expectations of Python's built-in behavior. For example, `__eq__` should return a boolean value (True or False), and `__str__` should return a human-readable string.
3. **Performance considerations**: Some magic methods, such as `__add__`, can create new objects. Ensure that the performance implications are well understood, especially in tight loops or performance-critical code.
4. **Intuitive behavior**: Make sure that your class behaves in a way that's intuitive for the user. For example, overloading `__add__` for a `Vector` class should result in adding vectors in a way that users expect from basic vector arithmetic.

Making Your Classes Intuitive and Pythonic

Using magic methods and operator overloading allows your classes to behave more like Python's built-in types. This not only makes your code cleaner and more intuitive but also enhances the overall user experience.

By providing customized behaviors for common operators and functions, you ensure that your class integrates seamlessly into Python's ecosystem. When done correctly, your class will feel **Pythonic**, meaning it will have a natural, consistent interface that feels like it was designed by a Python expert.

Summary

In this chapter, we covered the following key concepts:

- **Magic methods (dunder methods)** allow you to customize the behavior of your objects when interacting with

Python's built-in functions and operators.

- Common magic methods like `__str__`, `__repr__`, `__len__`, and `__eq__` provide essential functionality for displaying, comparing, and working with objects.
- **Operator overloading** allows you to redefine the behavior of operators like +, -, and * for your custom classes, making them work seamlessly with these familiar operators.
- Following best practices ensures that your magic methods make your classes more intuitive and Pythonic, leading to cleaner and more maintainable code.

In the next chapter, we will dive deeper into **Inheritance**, examining how it allows us to extend and reuse class functionality, making our programs more efficient and scalable.

Chapter 8: OOP in Real-World Applications

Object-Oriented Programming (OOP) is not just an academic concept—it's a powerful methodology that is widely applied in real-world software development. With OOP, you can model complex systems and develop software that is more modular, reusable, and maintainable. In this chapter, we will look at how OOP principles can be applied in practical, real-world applications, such as building address books, to-do list apps, and even integrating with databases. We will also explore how OOP enhances collaboration, scalability, and testing in large projects.

Applying OOP in Practical Scenarios

OOP provides the framework for modeling real-world entities and their interactions in software systems. Instead of working with raw functions and variables, OOP allows you to organize your code into objects—self-contained modules that combine both data and functionality. Each object is an instance of a class, and the class defines the properties (attributes) and behaviors (methods) that all instances of that class will share.

For example, in a **to-do list application**, you might have classes such as `Task`, `Category`, and `User`. Each `Task` would have attributes such as `name`, `due_date`, and `status`, while the `Category` class might hold attributes like `category_name` and a list of tasks. The `User` class could represent a user of the to-do list app, with methods to assign tasks to specific categories and users. By organizing your application this way, you make it easier to maintain, extend, and test.

Let's explore a few examples of how OOP can be implemented in real-world applications.

Let's consider building a **simple address book** using OOP. In a basic address book, we might want to store information about people, such as their name, address, phone number, and email. Using OOP, we can create a class that represents a **Contact**, with methods to add, remove, and display contacts.

Here's an example:

```python
CopyEdit
class Contact:
    def __init__(self, name, phone, email, address):
        self.name = name
        self.phone = phone
        self.email = email
        self.address = address

    def __str__(self):
        return f"{self.name}, {self.phone}, {self.email}, {self.address}"


class AddressBook:
    def __init__(self):
        self.contacts = []
```

```python
    def add_contact(self, contact):

self.contacts.append(contact)

    def display_contacts(self):
        for contact in
self.contacts:
            print(contact)


# Example usage
address_book = AddressBook()
contact1 = Contact("John Doe",
"555-1234", "john@example.com",
"123 Elm Street")
contact2 = Contact("Jane Smith",
"555-5678", "jane@example.com",
"456 Oak Avenue")

address_book.add_contact(contact1)
address_book.add_contact(contact2)

address_book.display_contacts()
```

Output:

```
nginx
CopyEdit
John Doe, 555-1234,
john@example.com, 123 Elm Street
Jane Smith, 555-5678,
jane@example.com, 456 Oak Avenue
```

In this example:

- The `Contact` class defines the attributes and methods related to a contact, such as storing the name, phone number, and email.
- The `AddressBook` class manages a list of contacts, with methods to add new contacts and display all stored contacts.

The OOP structure helps to encapsulate data and functionality in clear, organized components, making the system easy to extend. For instance, you could later add methods for searching, sorting, or deleting contacts.

How OOP Helps in Scalability, Testing, and Collaboration

One of the most significant advantages of OOP is its ability to support **scalable** development. In a real-world application, especially as it grows, the need for maintainability and flexibility becomes paramount. By using classes and objects, OOP allows your application to evolve more naturally over time.

Scalability

As your project scales, you can continue to build on top of existing classes without having to completely rewrite or restructure your code. This is particularly helpful when adding new features or expanding functionality. For instance, in a larger address book or to-do list app, you could extend the `Contact` class to include attributes for birthday reminders or an option to categorize contacts. By maintaining clean, modular code, you can keep the structure manageable as your project grows.

Testing

OOP also enhances testing. By isolating functionality in specific methods and classes, you can test components in isolation. If you're writing unit tests, you can test each class independently, ensuring that each part of your application behaves correctly before combining them into the larger system.

For example, in the address book app, you could write unit tests to ensure the `add_contact` method correctly adds a new contact to the list. You could test edge cases, like trying to add a duplicate contact or a contact with missing information, without worrying about the rest of the application.

Collaboration

In larger projects, teams of developers often work on different parts of the system. OOP allows multiple developers to work on different classes simultaneously, making it easier to collaborate. Each developer can focus on creating and testing one part of the application while ensuring that the rest of the system remains intact. Classes also make it easier to document the system, providing clear boundaries between different parts of the application.

Using OOP with File Handling and Basic Databases

OOP shines when working with persistent data storage. In many real-world applications, such as an address book or to-do list app, data is saved to a file or database. By encapsulating file handling and database access within classes, OOP makes it easier to manage this complexity.

Let's extend the **AddressBook** example to include file handling. In this case, we'll save contacts to a text file.

```python
CopyEdit
import pickle

class AddressBook:
    def __init__(self):
        self.contacts = []

    def add_contact(self, contact):

self.contacts.append(contact)

    def display_contacts(self):
        for contact in
self.contacts:
            print(contact)
```

```python
    def save_to_file(self,
filename):
        with open(filename, 'wb')
as file:

pickle.dump(self.contacts, file)

    def load_from_file(self,
filename):
        try:
            with open(filename,
'rb') as file:
                self.contacts =
pickle.load(file)
        except FileNotFoundError:
            print("No file found,
starting with an empty address
book.")

# Example usage
address_book = AddressBook()
address_book.add_contact(Contact("J
ohn Doe", "555-1234",
"john@example.com", "123 Elm
Street"))
address_book.save_to_file("contacts
.pkl")

new_address_book = AddressBook()
new_address_book.load_from_file("co
ntacts.pkl")
new_address_book.display_contacts()
```

In this example:

- The `save_to file` method serializes the list of contacts using the `pickle` module.
- The `load_from_file` method deserializes the contact data back into the address book.

This approach encapsulates file handling logic within the `AddressBook` class, making it easier to read and write data without needing to worry about low-level file operations elsewhere in your code.

Introduction to GUI with Tkinter Using OOP

Another great way to apply OOP is by creating **graphical user interfaces (GUIs)**. Python's `Tkinter` library is often used for simple desktop applications. By using OOP, you can organize your GUI components (buttons, text boxes, labels) into objects, each with its own attributes and behaviors.

Here's an example of how you might create a simple to-do list application with a GUI using OOP principles:

101

```python
python
CopyEdit
import tkinter as tk

class ToDoApp:
    def __init__(self, root):
        self.root = root
        self.root.title("To-Do List
App")

        self.tasks = []

        self.task_entry =
tk.Entry(root)
        self.task_entry.pack()

        self.add_button =
tk.Button(root, text="Add Task",
command=self.add_task)
        self.add_button.pack()

        self.tasks_listbox =
tk.Listbox(root)
        self.tasks_listbox.pack()

    def add_task(self):
        task =
self.task_entry.get()
        if task:
            self.tasks.append(task)
            self.update_task_list()

    def update_task_list(self):

self.tasks_listbox.delete(0,
tk.END)
        for task in self.tasks:
```

```
self.tasks_listbox.insert(tk.END,
task)

# Example usage
root = tk.Tk()
app = ToDoApp(root)
root.mainloop()
```

In this simple application:

- The `ToDoApp` class encapsulates the GUI components and the logic for adding tasks to the list.
- The `add_task` method adds a task to the `tasks` list and updates the display.
- The `update_task_list` method refreshes the list box to show the current tasks.

By organizing the GUI components as objects with their own behaviors and attributes, OOP helps maintain clean and modular code, even for graphical applications.

One of the primary advantages of OOP is **modularity**. By splitting a system into independent, self-contained classes, OOP allows you to break down complex problems into smaller, manageable pieces. Each class has a clear responsibility, and its internal logic is encapsulated, making it easier to understand, modify, and extend.

For example, in a to-do list app, you could separate the logic into different classes: `Task`, `Category`, and `User`. This modularity ensures that changes to one part of the system won't break the others. You can also test, debug, and develop each class in isolation, improving productivity and reducing errors.

Furthermore, OOP enhances **readability** by using **descriptive class and method names** that convey the intent of the code. This makes the codebase more approachable for new developers, improving collaboration and maintaining long-term sustainability.

Summary

In this chapter, we explored how Object-Oriented Programming (OOP) can be applied in real-world scenarios such as building address books, to-do list apps, and more. We highlighted the advantages of OOP, including:

- **Scalability**: Making it easier to grow and extend applications.
- **Testing**: Isolating components for effective unit testing.
- **Collaboration**: Enabling multiple developers to work on different parts of the system simultaneously.
- **File handling and databases**: Encapsulating data storage and retrieval logic.
- **GUI development**: Using OOP principles to design user interfaces.

By leveraging OOP in your projects, you'll be able to create more maintainable, readable, and scalable software systems, paving the way for more complex applications in the future.

In the next chapter, we will dive deeper into **Design Patterns**, which offer reusable solutions to common design problems in OOP. Stay tuned!

Chapter 9: Best Practices, Pitfalls, and Next Steps

As you continue to build your proficiency with Object-Oriented Programming (OOP) in Python, it's essential to understand not only the theory and application of OOP but also the best practices and common mistakes that can hinder your progress. In this chapter, we'll discuss the most common pitfalls for beginners, best practices for class design and naming conventions, and provide an introduction to unit testing. We'll also explore a few well-known OOP design patterns, and finally, we'll look at some advanced OOP concepts and the next steps in your Python journey.

Common Mistakes Beginners Make with OOP in Python

While OOP is a powerful paradigm, it can also be a source of frustration for beginners who are unfamiliar with its core principles.

Here are some of the most common mistakes and how to avoid them:

1. Overusing Inheritance

Inheritance is a fundamental OOP concept, but many beginners fall into the trap of using it excessively. They may create overly complex class hierarchies that add unnecessary layers to the code. While inheritance is useful for code reuse, overusing it can lead to tightly coupled classes and a lack of flexibility. It's important to remember that **composition** (using "has-a" relationships) can often be a better choice than inheritance, as it leads to more maintainable and flexible code.

2. Misunderstanding Encapsulation

Encapsulation is about keeping data safe from unintended modifications by using private and protected attributes. Beginners often make the mistake of exposing too many attributes or neglecting to use getter and setter methods. This leads to **data corruption** or **bugs** that are difficult to trace. It's best to keep your attributes private and provide controlled access via public methods or properties.

3. Neglecting Code Reusability

A key advantage of OOP is code reuse. Beginners often create new classes and functions for every small task without considering how code could be reused. Before writing new code, ask yourself: "Can I extend an existing class? Can I create a more generic solution?"

4. Not Using Polymorphism Effectively

Polymorphism allows objects of different types to be treated as instances of a common parent class. Beginners often overlook this powerful feature and write redundant or overly complex code. Understanding polymorphism helps reduce duplication and make the codebase easier to maintain.

5. Forgetting to Document Your Code

As you build more complex systems, documentation becomes critical. Beginners often skip docstrings and comments, making it difficult for others (or even themselves) to understand the logic later. Document your classes, methods, and functions to clarify their purpose and usage.

Best Practices for Class Design, Naming, and Documentation

Following good practices in OOP not only improves the quality of your code but also makes it easier for others to work with your codebase. Let's discuss best practices for designing classes, naming conventions, and documenting your code.

1. Class Design

A well-designed class should represent a clear, cohesive entity. Here are some tips:

- **Single Responsibility Principle (SRP):** Each class should have one responsibility. If your class is doing too much, it likely needs to be split into multiple smaller classes.
- **Modular Design:** Keep your classes modular. If a class grows too large, it can become difficult to maintain. Break it down into smaller classes and use composition where possible.
- **Use Inheritance Appropriately:** Use inheritance when you have a true "is-a" relationship between classes (for example, a `Car` is a type of `Vehicle`). For anything else, consider using composition (has-a relationships) instead.

2. Naming Conventions

Naming your classes and methods clearly and consistently is crucial for readability:

- **Class Names:** Use **CamelCase** for class names. For example, `CustomerProfile`, `OrderDetails`.
- **Method and Function Names:** Use **snake_case** for method names. For example, `calculate_total`, `send_email`.

- **Avoid Ambiguous Names:** Use descriptive names that make it clear what each class or method does. For example, a class that represents a user profile should be named `UserProfile`, not just `Profile`.

3. Documentation

Every class, method, and function should have a docstring explaining what it does, its parameters, and its return value. This is particularly helpful for future developers (or yourself) who will work with your code.

- **Class Docstrings:** Describe the class's purpose and any important methods or attributes.
- **Method Docstrings:** Include descriptions of the method's parameters and return values.

Here's an example of a well-documented class:

```python
CopyEdit
class Product:
    """
    A class that represents a
product in an inventory system.
```

```
    Attributes:
    name (str): The name of the
product.
    price (float): The price of the
product.
    stock (int): The number of
items in stock.

    Methods:
    update_stock(amount): Updates
the stock level of the product.
    get_product_info(): Returns the
product's details as a dictionary.
    """
    def __init__(self, name, price,
stock):
        self.name = name
        self.price = price
        self.stock = stock

    def update_stock(self, amount):
        """Updates the stock level
by the given amount."""
        self.stock += amount

    def get_product_info(self):
        """Returns a dictionary of
the product details."""
        return {"name": self.name,
"price": self.price, "stock":
self.stock}
```

Testing is an essential part of OOP to ensure that your classes and methods behave as expected. Python's built-in `unittest` module or the third-party `pytest` library are great tools for writing tests for your OOP code.

Writing Tests with `unittest`

To test an OOP-based application, you can write unit tests for each class and its methods. Here's an example:

```python
CopyEdit
import unittest

class TestProduct(unittest.TestCase):
    def setUp(self):
        """Set up any data needed for the tests."""
        self.product = Product("Laptop", 1000.0, 50)

    def test_update_stock(self):
        """Test the update_stock method."""
```

```python
        self.product.update_stock(20)

        self.assertEqual(self.product.stock
, 70)

    def
test_get_product_info(self):
        """Test the
get_product_info method."""
        expected_info = {"name":
"Laptop", "price": 1000.0, "stock":
50}

        self.assertEqual(self.product.get_p
roduct_info(), expected_info)

if __name__ == "__main__":
    unittest.main()
```

Here:

- `setUp()` sets up any objects or data needed for the tests.
- `test_update_stock()` checks that the stock updates correctly when a new amount is added.
- `test_get_product_info()` verifies that the product's information is returned accurately.

Writing Tests with `pytest`

`pytest` provides a simpler, more concise syntax for writing tests:

```python
CopyEdit
import pytest

@pytest.fixture
def product():
    return Product("Laptop", 1000.0, 50)

def test_update_stock(product):
    product.update_stock(20)
    assert product.stock == 70

def test_get_product_info(product):
    expected_info = {"name": "Laptop", "price": 1000.0, "stock": 50}
    assert product.get_product_info() == expected_info
```

Here, `pytest` automatically detects the `product` fixture and injects it into the test functions.

Design patterns are reusable solutions to common problems that occur in software design. Some of the most commonly used OOP design patterns include:

1. Singleton Pattern

This pattern ensures that a class has only one instance and provides a global access point to it. For example, a database connection class might use the Singleton pattern to ensure that only one connection is created during the lifetime of the application.

```python
CopyEdit
class Singleton:
    _instance = None

    def __new__(cls):
        if cls._instance is None:
            cls._instance =
super(Singleton, cls).__new__(cls)
        return cls._instance
```

2. Factory Pattern

The Factory pattern defines an interface for creating objects, but allows subclasses to alter the type of objects that will be created. This is useful when you need to create different types of objects based on some condition.

```python
CopyEdit
class Animal:
    def speak(self):
        pass

class Dog(Animal):
    def speak(self):
        return "Woof"

class Cat(Animal):
    def speak(self):
        return "Meow"

class AnimalFactory:
    def create_animal(self,
animal_type):
        if animal_type == "dog":
            return Dog()
        elif animal_type == "cat":
            return Cat()
```

Intro to Advanced OOP: Mixins, Decorators, Metaclasses

Once you're comfortable with the basics of OOP, you can explore more advanced topics:

1. MIxins

A mixin is a class that provides methods to other classes but isn't meant to stand on its own. Mixins allow you to add reusable functionality across multiple classes.

2. Decorators

Decorators are functions that modify the behavior of other functions or methods. In OOP, they can be used to add functionality to methods or to manage access control.

3. Metaclasses

Metaclasses define the behavior of classes themselves. They allow you to customize the creation of new classes and modify their behavior dynamically.

What's Next: Building Projects, Frameworks (Django, Flask), and Career Growth

Now that you've built a solid foundation in OOP, the next step is to apply what you've learned by building real-world projects. Consider creating applications using popular Python frameworks like **Django** and **Flask** for web development. These frameworks are built on OOP principles and will help you expand your skills.

Additionally, continue to explore more advanced Python topics, and focus on **career growth**. Practice building larger systems, contribute to open-source projects, and start learning about software architecture and design principles.

www.ingramcontent.com/pod-product-compliance
Lightning Source LLC
La Vergne TN
LVHW051702050326
832903LV00032B/3952